"Your emotions are
a guide. They show you
what is important to
you and what matters
to you."

—SUNITA RAY, PSYD

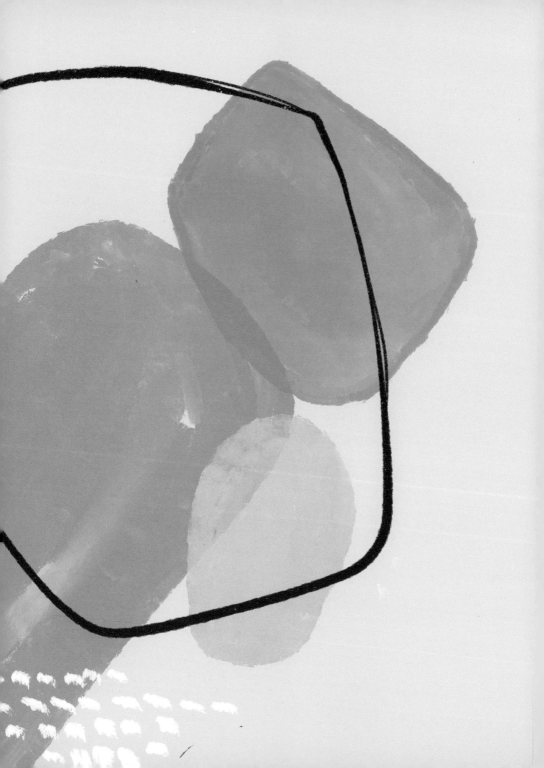

embrace your emotions

a self-care journal to discover the wisdom of your feelings

Jennifer King Lindley

foreword by Sarah Smith
Editor-in-Chief of *Prevention*

HEARST
HOME

contents

welcome to your feelings

Anger. Embarrassment. Envy. I've felt all of these things—not just in my life, but in the last week. How about you? Has it been all happiness and light, or are you human like me? I can feel such joy one moment—like, laughing with my family at the dinner table—and then three other less attractive emotions before we even clear the plates. *(No one's going to ask me about my day?!)*

I don't think we talk enough about those so-called "negative" emotions: the ones that don't make it to social media, the ones that many of us are accustomed to tamping down, the ones that make us feel like we're doing something wrong.

We aren't, though. I once read one of those click-bait-y articles about a woman who never smiled because she didn't want to get wrinkles. It's heartbreaking, right? No chuckling at a dumb joke, no lighting up when you see a friend, no smiling in your vacation photos. We can all pretty much agree that depriving yourself like that leaves life with a huge hole in it. But downplaying our more difficult emotions is a loss too. Feeling hurt or rejected, angry or embarrassed: These things indicate that we are alive. We are putting ourselves out into the world and taking part in all of its joys and sorrows. Feeling all the emotions and taking the right cues from them means living a full life.

That's why I think this book is so valuable. It's an insightful guidebook to our emotions and our feelings about our feelings—and it's also a workbook, so you can really dig in to how it all works for you. This book is designed to help you recognize and connect with a wide range of feelings and understand the purpose they play in your life. Gratitude is in here—and hope—but you'll also be pushed to think about what you might consider more unsavory emotions, like fear and shame. Get a pencil, because the real power comes from answering the prompts about the mix of emotions that makes your life so enriching.

I love this book because it offers a different experience for each and every person who cracks it open and takes its message to heart: Life is richer when you experience a rainbow of emotions. So, explore these pages at your own pace. Learn what there is to know about living a full-color life, then fill in the blanks...with *your* story.

Sarah

Editor-in-Chief, *Prevention*

how are you feeling?

Take a moment right now to check in with yourself. Chances are your answer is "OK, I guess," "Blah," or—most likely—"Hmmm. I don't know!" Most of us ignore our emotions unless they are absolutely screaming. The chatter of our busy brains or the distraction of an endless to-do list often drown out our feelings. When we do tune in to them, we may struggle to put into words how we feel or judge ourselves harshly for having the "wrong" emotions. ("It is so small of me to feel envious of my best friend!")

Adding to the confusion: The current culture of toxic positivity views some of our emotions as unacceptable. *Good vibes only!* Grief, regret, or disappointment are signs that something is wrong and needs fixing...unnecessary detours on our rightful path to constant joy. "There is pressure to think, *I have so much to feel grateful for, I don't have the right to be sad,*" says therapist Whitney Goodman, author of *Toxic Positivity: Keeping It Real in a World Obsessed with Being Happy.* "But denying your feelings creates inner turmoil and shame that keeps you stuck."

In fact, all our emotions—the good, the bad, the ugly—can be powerful sources of wisdom and insight if we learn to attend to them. A new field of research into "emodiversity" is finding that experiencing a wide range of emotions each day, both positive and negative, is the road to greatest well-being. A groundbreaking study of 37,000 subjects published in the *Journal of Experimental Psychology* found people who reported experiencing a wide variety of emotions in their daily lives were physically and mentally healthier compared to those who could only cite a few feelings.

THE POWER OF JOURNALING

Throughout this guide, you are invited to put pen to paper, feelings into words. This kind of expressive writing has powerful benefits. In a series of influential studies, James Pennebaker, Ph.D., a professor of psychology at the University of Texas at Austin, asked subjects to spend 15 minutes a day for four days writing about their most painful experience—the death of a loved one, an estrangement, an illness. They were asked to pour out their deepest emotions and reflect on how that difficult time had shaped other aspects of their life— their past, their current relationships, their career. Across studies, those who took part in this kind of writing show a host of benefits, from less depression to fewer doctor's visits. Why might the simple act of writing confer such benefits? Writing may help you reframe an event in a meaningful way and make sense of it. It helps you weave experiences into your own unique life story—as you will do throughout this guide.

"Emotions are messengers. Even the ones that we don't like are trying to let us know something about what we need. If we ignore those messages, it will impact our relationships, our sleep, our productivity," explains Charryse Johnson, Ph.D., L.C.M.H.C., founder of Jade Integrative Counseling and Wellness.

The good news: Understanding and managing our feelings are skills we can all get better at. The expert tips and thought-provoking prompts in this journal are based on the latest research into the growing field of emotional intelligence.

Dip into the exercises and you can tap into the rich wellspring of *all* your emotions. You will become more skillful in identifying what you are feeling and why. The payoffs are many: When you gain greater understanding, you access wisdom that can help you maintain closer relationships, clarify your values, and manage your most intense feelings when you are overwhelmed.

Exuberance! Delight! Relief! Emotions come in all the shades of the ginormous crayon box. They give life its vivid richness. Working through the exercises in this book will help you embrace all your emotions.

In doing so, you can, at last, create your full-color life.

"Our feelings are our most genuine paths to knowledge."

—AUDRE LORDE

START WHERE YOU ARE

what *are* emotions?

Imagine for a moment what your life would be like without emotions. Sure, you would have no aching grief or crushing disappointment, but also no transcendent joy or goose-bump awe. Wouldn't life be *blah*?

You feel emotions all day, every day, but you may struggle to put into words what these elusive sensations are. For something so basic to human experience, researchers themselves are still puzzling out the mysteries of emotions and how they serve us.

"Emotions drive a lot of our thinking and behavior," says Jessica Tracy, Ph.D., professor of psychology and director of the Emotions & Self Lab at the University of British Columbia. In fact, at one point in our evolutionary history, emotions were nothing short of a matter of life or death. They evolved as powerful guidance systems that helped us survive by activating our minds and our bodies in specific ways, she explains. For example: Picture your long-ago ancestor happily gathering berries when suddenly a lion leaps into view. Shot through with a jolt of fear, her heart rate jumps, stress hormones surge, and eyes widen to ready for action. Her thoughts become laser-focused on escape. Similarly, positive emotions like compassion and love helped us get along with our tribe and care for our offspring—both essential for survival.

Our modern world is a lot more complicated. Now the trigger that gets our hearts pumping and brains spinning is not a lion but a volley of urgent emails or an endless traffic jam. Yet these same emotions continue to shape our current experience in profound ways.

One thing is certain: Emotions are infinitely complex and wide open to our interpretation. "I describe emotions as body sensations with a story attached to them," says Britt Frank, L.S.C.S.W., a clinician and author of *The Science of Stuck: Breaking Through Inertia to Find Your Path Forward.* "If I have a pit in my stomach, sweaty palms, and a dry mouth, those are body sensations. If I'm going to go on a date with someone I really like, I describe those sensations to myself as excitement. But if I am feeling that way while I am readying for a job interview, I describe my feelings as anxiety." Emotions may come and go in minutes, and we may have several overlapping at the same time, she says. It's no wonder we find them so confusing!

Take time to reflect on your current relationship with your emotions and the role they have played in your life so far.

"The best and most beautiful things in the world cannot be seen or even touched. They must be felt with the heart."

—HELEN KELLER

Tune In

Children are typically very in touch with their emotions. (Just watch a preschooler drop their ice-cream cone.) Tap into your emotional memory bank and write about a vivid experience from childhood when you felt an intense emotion.

....

....

....

....

....

....

....

....

....

....

....

....

....

....

....

....

....

TRY THIS

How you describe your inner experiences to yourself can have a big impact on how you feel, advises Melody Wilding, L.M.S.W., executive coach and author of *Trust Yourself.*

Next time you are feeling overwhelmed, don't ratchet up your stress even further by telling yourself, "OMG, I AM GOING CRAZY! THIS WILL LAST FOREVER!!!"

Instead, step back and try to name the emotion in a word. "I am feeling... anxious." Noting the emotion helps you realize it is simply a passing feeling, common enough to have a familiar name. "Labeling the emotion creates distance and gives you a sense of control," she explains.

Catch Feelings

Simply pausing in your day and intentionally reflecting on your feelings can get you in touch with them. Stop once a day this week and write about what you are feeling.

SUNDAY ....

....

....

....

....

....

....

....

MONDAY ....

....

....

....

....

....

....

Hint Setting a reminder on your phone for the same time every day can help you keep at it.

....

....

....

TUESDAY ....

....

....

....

....

....

....

....

....

....

WEDNESDAY ....

....

....

....

....

....

....

....

....

.... **Continued** ⟶

THURSDAY ....

....

....

....

....

....

....

....

....

FRIDAY ....

....

....

....

....

....

....

....

....

....

....

....

....

....

....

....

....

....

....

....

Reflect

Look back on your feelings for the week. Do you notice any patterns?

....

....

....

....

....

....

Draw Out Your Feelings

If you want to get in closer touch with your emotions, get creative! "Art can give us another language to explore our feelings," says Paige Scheinberg, M.S., A.T.R.-B.C, an integrative art therapist and founder of SHINE ON Consulting (@shineonwithpaige). "We can express ourselves through color and shape and release our feelings onto paper."

Don't worry if you're not a natural Picasso. Here are her tips for where to begin—and some space to give it a whirl!

Choose your materials. You don't want to break out the complicated oil paints and turpentine on your first try. "Use materials you are comfortable with. For adult beginners, I suggest magic markers or colored pencils. Crayons can bring adults right back to childhood, which can be a positive or negative thing."

Start small. A huge blank canvas can be anxiety producing. Instead, "start on a little piece of paper or repurpose pages from a book or use old sheet music to draw on. That can be much less intimidating," says Scheinberg.

Take a few deep breaths. This helps you relax your body and mind and signals you are about to dive into the creative zone. "Remind yourself that this time is for you. There is no judgement, no right or wrong."

Follow your curiosity. Scheinberg suggests beginning to play with art and emotion by exploring a positive emotion like peacefulness or joy. As you draw, consider: What color will you use to express it? What shape might the emotion be? Does it have sharp or smooth edges? Can you draw an object that represents it?

Set a timer. To relieve the pressure of deciding when your art is "done," set a limit of three to five minutes. "As you look at what you have created, take time to honor and savor your creative process and the feeling your art represents for you."

Go deeper. Once you get comfortable, you can move on to explore more difficult emotions, like anger, if you wish.

What emotion are you feeling right now?
Practice drawing it on the opposite page!

Familial Feels

Growing up, what messages did you receive about emotions from your family? Did you talk openly about your feelings or were they brushed off? Were you supposed to keep a stiff upper lip? Was talking about emotions taboo? Did everyone just let loose?

....
....
....
....
....
....
....
....
....
....
....

TRY THIS

Reminder: Emotional regulation starts with good self-care. "You will handle life's ups and downs better with these basic strategies," says Kathy HoganBruen, Ph.D., clinical psychologist and founder of the District Anxiety Center in Washington, DC.

1. Make good sleep a priority.

2. Move your body through regular exercise you enjoy.

3. Nourish yourself with nutrient-packed foods.

4. Practice mindfulness or other spiritual practices you find meaningful.

5. Spend quality time with others.

Listen to Your Heart

Have you ever wept your way through a cheesy breakup song or
started instantly dancing with joy to a chart-topping hit? Take
advantage of music's powerful hold on emotions by playing
a favorite song. As you listen, free-write about the feelings it
brings up for you.

TRY THIS

One place to begin exploring your emotions is simply getting curious, suggests Jasmine Marie, CEO and founder of Black Girls Breathing and author of the forthcoming book *Black Girls Breathing*. "Give yourself permission to experience an emotion without the need to label it 'good' or 'bad' in the first place," she says. "If we can honor our feelings and observe them with nonattachment, we'd feel a lot less shame for having them."

Open Up to Others

Discussing our true feelings can be scary—we risk being judged or worry we will come off as a burden. When a friend asks, "How are you?" we often answer, "I'm fine," when in fact we are feeling anything but.

How would you honestly answer if a friend asked you this right now?

How would it feel to share your true feelings in this way?

I'M FINE

why do we avoid our emotions?

Alas, most of us are surprisingly bad at identifying what we are *really* feeling. In her pioneering work on shame and resilience, best-selling author Brené Brown, Ph.D., asked seven thousand subjects to keep a list of all the emotions they experienced. The average number was a measly three: happy, sad, and angry. That vanilla-only list leaves out the remarkably nuanced range of human feeling: shame, trepidation, ebullience, disgust...to name a few.

We fumble to understand our feelings for many reasons. We may have been raised to think being emotional is a sign of weakness—big girls don't cry. We might be hesitant to talk honestly about our feelings with others. ("How are you?" "I'm fine!") Plus, examining our feelings can be uncomfortable and even scary. What if we don't like what we discover?

It's natural to want to avoid opening a Pandora's box of bad feelings. Negative emotions can feel painful, and humans are wired to avoid pain. So we adopt avoidance strategies: We fill our online carts to the brim, pack our days in frenzied busyness, and dilute a hurt with a big goblet of merlot.

The problem: When you try to shove uncomfortable emotions down, they bounce back up like a beach ball you're scrambling to keep underwater. "By trying desperately to escape an emotion, you actually end up holding on to it harder," says Ronald Rogge, Ph.D., a professor of psychology at the University of Rochester. "You experience it a lot more intensely and suffer more as a result." Indeed, research has found that people who suppress their emotions are more prone to experience anxiety and depression.

Living in this constricted way means blunting your positive emotions too. As writer Jonathan Safran Foer said, "You cannot protect yourself from sadness without protecting yourself from happiness."

Let's investigate ways you might be—consciously or unconsciously—avoiding your own feelings.

"Until you make the unconscious conscious, it will direct your life and you will call it fate."

—C.G. JUNG

Reveal Your Anger Iceberg

Often our anger is self-protective, covering up vulnerable feelings that we have a hard time admitting, such as fear or shame. Therapists often call this the "anger iceberg," because we are not acknowledging what else we are feeling underneath the rage.

Write about something you are angry about.

....

....

....

....

What other emotions emerge as you write? Are there other emotions beneath your anger? Explore them here.

....

....

....

....

....

....

....

....

How Do You Numb Your Feelings?

Life is stressful! It's only natural to want to find ways to unwind. But are your go-to activities recharging—or just a way to numb out and avoid your feelings? For the next week, keep a log of your favorite distractions and reflect on how they are serving you.

Before I started, I felt...	My distraction
SUNDAY	
MONDAY	
TUESDAY	
WEDNESDAY	
THURSDAY	
FRIDAY	
SATURDAY	

Time spent	Afterward, I felt...

Continued ⟶

Reflect

Now reread your entries. Which of these distractions felt nourishing
to you? Which felt more like junk food? Can you use this information
to make different choices this week?

....

....

....

....

....

....

....

....

....

....

....

....

....

....

....

....

....

....

EMBARRASSMENT

We've all been there. The spinach wad in your front teeth. The awkward comment we want to immediately take back. The wardrobe malfunction. Feeling embarrassment makes us squirm and blush...and there's a good reason for it.

"As humans, we have evolved to live in groups. We are sometimes going to do things wrong that we didn't intend," explains Christine Harris, Ph.D., a professor of psychology at the University of California, San Diego. Looking embarrassed acts as a sort of physical apology to those around us, smoothing over our goofs and promoting harmony with others.

"Embarrassment is the emotion that says, 'Whoops! I messed up and I didn't mean to,'" says Harris. Across cultures, humans show this emotion with the same universal gestures, she notes—

we avert our gaze, tip our head, make a tight smile, touch our faces, and often blush.

Next time you feel embarrassed, remind yourself that everyone screws up from time to time. Plus, embarrassment loves company. In one study, researchers asked subjects to sing the '70s schmaltz standard "Feelings." ("Nothing more than feelings...") Those who were allowed to rate their level of embarrassment afterward by talking about it with a researcher felt immediate relief from their chagrin. Those who didn't have the chance to offload continued to feel cringey. "If you can laugh at yourself, it is always best," says Mary Lamia, Ph.D., a psychotherapist and author of Emotions!: Making Sense of Your Feelings. "And usually if you share an embarrassment, someone has a better one."

Avoid the Anxiety Snowball Effect

"We make our negative emotions bigger by avoiding them," explains Amelia Aldao, Ph.D., founder and director of Together CBT. "Say I am dreading small talk at a party. If I stay home, I feel immediate relief. But without the chance to experience this kind of chitchat and live through it, small talk now makes me more anxious. The more we avoid, the less we allow ourselves to feel our feelings, the more scared we become of these feelings. It is a snowball."

1 **What have you avoided doing recently because of fear or discomfort? What was bothering you about it?**

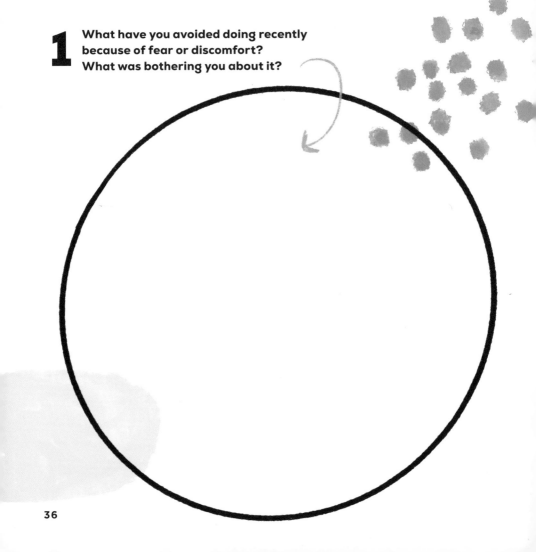

2 How did you feel immediately after refusing or canceling?

Continued ⟶

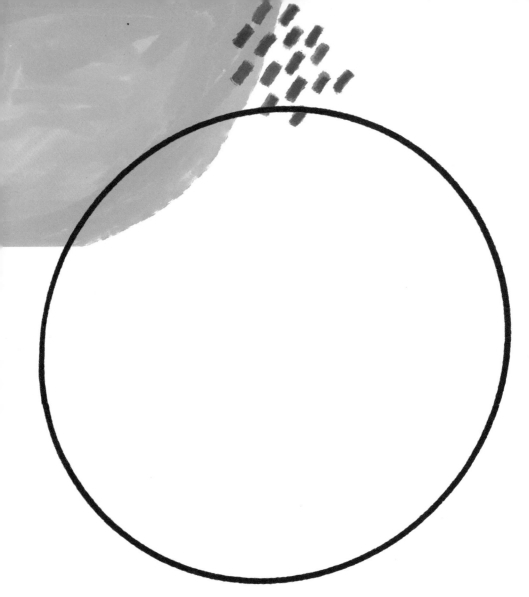

3 How did you feel about avoiding that activity when you thought about it the next day?

4 Is there a way you could handle this situation differently the next time? How might that feel?

Identify Your "Go-to" Emotion

People often have a "dominant emotion," such as anxiety or anger, notes Alice Boyes, Ph.D., author of *The Healthy Mind Toolkit*. "They channel all their energy and focus into that one emotion, partly because it helps them avoid other, less familiar feelings, like regret," she says.

What is your "go-to" emotion?
Write about a current experience that is making you feel this way.

....

....

....

....

....

....

....

....

....

....

....

....

....

....

....

Shush Your Inner Critic

We often censor our own emotions, thinking we don't have a right to feel a certain way. *(I shouldn't be disappointed to not get that big promotion. I am lucky to have a job!)*

Write about a time you told yourself you shouldn't feel a certain way.

....

....

....

....

....

....

....

....

Did you feel better or worse after telling yourself this? Why?

....

....

....

....

....

....

....

....

Now, let's be honest, how would you state your real feelings if there were no shoulds involved?

....

....

....

....

....

....

....

....

....

....

....

....

....

....

....

....

TRY THIS

Having something always blasting in your ears can be one way of avoiding your emotions, notes Boyes. If you feel antsy going for a walk, driving, or enduring a plane ride without a podcast or playlist, this might be an issue for you. Next time you take a long walk, leave those earbuds at home. Pay attention to the thoughts and feelings that come up for you during your stroll. Does anything you experience surprise you? Then pause and reflect. Are there other emotions that might be lurking underneath this big one? Try to sift and find at least one.

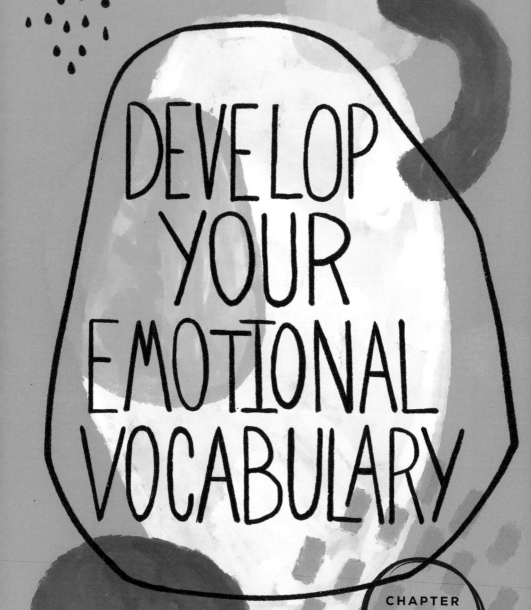

DEVELOP YOUR EMOTIONAL VOCABULARY

CHAPTER
3

how to identity what you are *really* feeling

You might have a vague sense you are feeling great—but what flavor of great? Amused, joyful, tranquil? Or bad—resentful, envious, disappointed? While it may not always come naturally, learning to distinguish among your feelings and identify their many variations is a skill we can all sharpen. Researchers even have a term for this ability: "emotional granularity."

According to a study published in the journal *Emotion*, individuals who are more aware of their precise emotions—who know they are feeling not just vaguely awful but *irritated*—tend to report higher levels of well-being and life satisfaction.

Why is pinpointing what you are feeling so helpful? "Name it to tame it" is a classic therapy mantra. Labeling an emotion "transfers some of the energy from the emotional side of our brain to our prefrontal cortex, the thinking part of our brain, so we are able to consider our situation more rationally," says Laura Silberstein-Tirch, Ph.D., director of the Center for Compassion Focused Therapy in New York City.

Plus, identifying the exact emotion we are feeling in turn can guide us to the best response: Do your flipping stomach and sweaty palms mean you are *anxious*...or *overwhelmed*? "If you're snapping at your in-laws because you're *anxious*, for example, you can decide to take yourself out for a soothing walk," says Amelia Aldao, Ph.D., founder and director of Together CBT. "If you are snapping because you are *overwhelmed* by having to get everything ready for the holidays, you can ask others to pitch in."

It works the same way with positive emotions. You may feel "good" about a recent job offer. But pause and ponder—are you *thrilled* by the challenge or simply *relieved* you found something so you can pay the mortgage? Being able to discriminate the type of good feeling you have can provide insights that will help guide your career decisions going forward.

Boosting your own emotional literacy can start with the basics, like making a practice of checking in with your body—are you feeling tension or discomfort somewhere? Tight shoulders or prickling skin? Referring to an emotion chart, such as the one on page 48 and 49, can also become a springboard of self-inquiry, helping you put words to feelings, says Jessica Borelli, Ph.D., professor of psychological science at the University of California, Irvine, and author of *Nature Meets Nurture: Science-Based Strategies for Raising Resilient Kids*. Practice when you are not totally overwhelmed. "I have feeling charts posted on mirrors around my home. Often when I brush my teeth at night, I will contemplate, *What did I feel today?*" says Borelli. "I also use these charts to cultivate this skill with my kids."

Dip into the following pages to become a connoisseur of your own nuanced feelings.

Let's Practice

What big emotion from the Feelings Word List on pages 48 and 49 might you be feeling right now? Refer to the top six core emotions.

....

....

....

....

....

....

Can you move down the list and identify what you are feeling more precisely?

....

....

....

....

....

Are there additional emotions from this list you are feeling right now too?

....

....

....

....

....

FEELINGS WORD LIST

Happy	Mad	Sad
Adored	Aggravated	Alone
Alive	Accused	Blue
Appreciated	Angry	Burdened
Cheerful	Bitter	Depressed
Ecstatic	Cross	Devasted
Excited	Defensive	Disappointed
Grateful	Frustrated	Discouraged
Glad	Furious	Grief-stricken
Hopeful	Hostile	Gloomy
Jolly	Impatient	Hopeless
Jovial	Infuriated	Let down
Joyful	Insulted	Lonely
Loved	Offended	Heartbroken
Merry	Ornery	Melancholy
Optimistic	Outraged	Miserable
Pleased	Pestered	Neglected
Satisfied	Rebellious	Pessimistic
Tender	Resistant	Remorseful
Terrific	Revengeful	Resentful
Thankful	Scorned	Solemn
Uplifted	Spiteful	Threatened
Warm	Testy	
	Violated	

Scared	Surprise	Disgust
Afraid	Astonished	Embarrassed
Alarm	Curious	Exposed
Anxious	Delighted	Guilty
Bashful	Enlightened	Ignored
Cautious	Exhilarated	Inadequate
Fearful	Incredulous	Incompetent
Frightened	Inquisitive	Inhibited
Horrified	Impressed	Inept
Lost	Mystified	Inferior
Haunted	Passionate	Insignificant
Helpless	Playful	Sick
Hesitant	Replenished	Shame
Insecure	Splendid	Squashed
Nervous	Shocked	Stupid
Petrified	Stunned	Ugly
Puzzled		Unaccepted
Reassured		
Reserved		
Sheepish		
Tearful		
Uncomfortable		
Useless		

TRY THIS

Practice a Compassionate Body Scan

"Emotions are held in the body. There's a direct connection between what's happening physically and what's happening psychologically," explains Charryse Johnson, Ph.D., L.C.M.H.C., founder of Jade Integrative Counseling and Wellness. "You might say you are *fine*, but your body will tell the truth. You might have a backache from stress or feel sick to your stomach from anger."

To get in better touch with your emotions, Johnson suggests doing a compassionate body scan, investigating your sensations without judgment.

1 Close your eyes. Start at the top of your head, and then go down little by little at a pace that feels comfortable for you: head nose, cheeks, chin, vertebra by vertebra, all the way down to your toes.

2 Notice any sensations as you go. "Are you holding any tightness or tension? Aches or prickles? If so, ask yourself how long has that been there? Did I feel that when I woke up this morning? Do I only feel that after I'm around certain people or in certain situations?"

3 You might be inclined to try to banish uncomfortable sensations or criticize yourself for not feeling differently. "Instead, ask yourself: *What are these sensations telling me I need? I might need to talk to an empathetic friend, I might need time to be alone and unwind, I might need bodywork to release all the tension in my shoulders.*" Gentle listening can help you be kind to yourself.

What did you discover during your body scan?
Describe the sensations by drawing or writing on the outline below.

Embrace Change

To experience a wider range of emotions, get out of your daily routine.
You don't have to take up scuba diving or fly off to New Zealand! You could
attend a local concert, explore a new neighborhood, or try a new hobby.

What did you try today that you have never done before?

....

....

....

....

....

....

....

How did that make you feel?

....

....

....

....

....

....

....

What happy detour from life could you take tomorrow?

....

....

....

....

....

....

....

....

....

"Sometimes I have kept my feelings to myself, because I could find no language to describe them."

—JANE AUSTEN

Follow Your Feelings

Set a reminder on your phone to check in about how you are feeling at the same time every day this week. You can refer to the feelings chart to help you. Consider these questions:

What are you feeling right now? What sensations do you feel in your body? What thoughts are going through your mind?

After checking in, dig deeper. Consider these questions and continue to write.

What is happening that might have triggered this emotion? Who are you with? What are you doing? Were you hungry, tired, dehydrated? (These are physical states that can negatively impact our mood say therapists.)

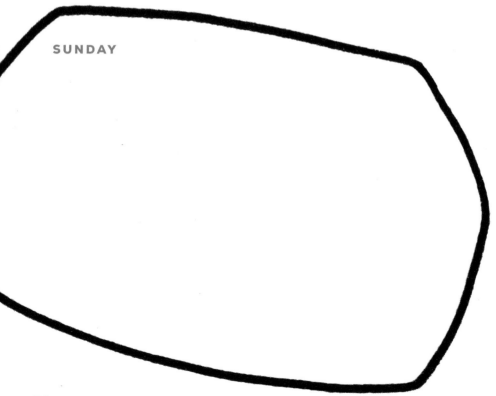

SUNDAY

MONDAY

TUESDAY

Continued ⟶

WEDNESDAY

THURSDAY

FRIDAY

SATURDAY

Get Personal

Emotions are universal, but we experience them very personally. Explore your current state using your senses and a little creativity.

I am feeling ....

....

....

If this emotion were a color, it would be... ....

....

....

....

....

....

....

If it was a sound, it would sound like... ....

....

....

....

....

....

....

....

If it was a taste, it would taste like... ....

....

....

....

....

....

....

....

....

....

If I could touch, it would feel like... ....

....

....

....

....

....

....

....

....

....

> # "Feelings come and go like clouds in a windy sky."
>
> —THICH NHAT HAHN

BOREDOM

It is a rainy Sunday afternoon. Time as you know it...has...completely...stopped. The feeling of boredom makes us uncomfortable, squirmy, restless. We're unable to focus our attention in any way that's satisfying. But boredom can also be a rich source of creativity if we can sit with it. When there's nothing riveting to occupy us, "it feels uncomfortable for the mind to be unengaged," says Teresa Belton, Ph.D., an academic associate at the School of Education and Lifelong Learning at the University of East Anglia who has researched boredom extensively. "If there appears to be nothing to do, we can be spurred into thinking in ways we might not otherwise think."

The mind wandering can be a perfect state for out-of-the box thinking. (Have you ever had revelations while zoning out in the shower, for instance?) So put down the darn phone and see what surprising places your mind takes you!

Having Mixed Emotions Is Totally Normal!

Though they rarely make Instagram-highlight reels, uncomfortable feelings are often part of even joyful times like weddings, holidays, or graduations. Acknowledging this simple reality can start to take the pressure off the occasion, says Aldao. "For instance, vacations are fun. But they are not fun 100 percent of the time. You might feel annoyed. You might feel exhausted. You might feel nervous."

Understanding it's natural to have a mix of feelings even on "happy" occasions means you won't be blindsided or declare the experience totally ruined. That makes you more open to the positives as well.

Contemplate a big event in your own life. What mix of emotions did you experience? Was one feeling bigger than the others during this important time? Divide the pie chart below to represent your mixed feelings.

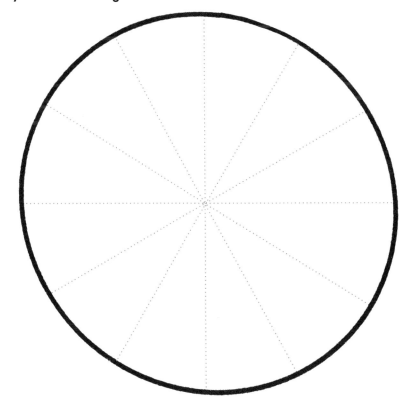

A Novel Idea

Beloved books can often help us access a flood of feelings. Write about a favorite book or a recent read that you found deeply moving. What emotions does it bring up for you?

....

....

....

....

....

....

....

....

....

....

....

"A book should serve as an axe for the frozen sea within us."

—FRANZ KAFKA

Write about a time you have felt something similar in your own life.

....

....

....

....

....

....

....

....

....

....

....

....

....

....

....

....

....

....

....

INVITE YOUR YOUR DEMONS TO TEA

CHAPTER
4

sitting with difficult emotions

Anger. Resentment. Jealousy. It's perfectly natural to want to ignore and deny our uncomfortable feelings. Those around us might insist on talking us out of them—"Come on, cheer up!" But that's a short-term fix at best. A more empowering strategy, say experts: Practice turning toward difficult feelings and looking them straight in the eye.

"So many people think that if they lean into their negative emotions, those emotions are going to get bigger," says Jessica Borelli, Ph.D., professor of psychological science at the University of California, Irvine, and author of *Nature Meets Nurture: Science-Based Strategies for Raising Resilient Kids*. "The opposite is true. The more you lean into these emotions, the less power they have. Doing so releases the tension that avoiding them creates. I always share with my clients the metaphor of the finger trap: The more you pull away, the tighter it gets."

Being brave enough to sit with your more difficult feelings allows you to "metabolize" them or work through them so they can dissipate. If you don't, they just holler louder as the needs that sparked them remain unaddressed. They may even surface as physical sensations such as stomach aches or depression, according to research.

Our uncomfortable emotions exist for a reason, explains Laura Silberstein-Tirch, Psy.D., director of the Center for Compassion Focused Therapy in New York City. "They are like an alarm system. They point us to important information, and they organize our minds and bodies to respond." Jealousy alerts us that something we love is at risk. Loneliness is a hunger that pushes us up off the coach and toward connection. These are important messages if we listen.

Remember: Accepting you are having these feelings doesn't mean you are accepting the circumstances that caused them, wallowing endlessly, or adopting a fatalistic attitude. Instead, acceptance helps you look for the *why* behind them and the *what* to do about them.

Difficult emotions are part of everyone's life. Here are some strategies for getting more comfortable with yours.

"Only in the darkness can you see the stars."

—MARTIN LUTHER KING JR.

➤ TRY THIS

Tune In With an Oceanic Breath

The simple act of breathing can be a powerful tool to get in touch with emotions we may be ignoring in the daily hustle and bustle. "Breath work allows us the opportunity to stay in the moment, breathe through our emotions, and affirm to ourselves that it's safe to feel," says Jasmine Marie, CEO and founder of Black Girls Breathing and author of the forthcoming book *Black Girls Breathing*. One helpful exercise for doing so is the Oceanic Breath. "Practice this regularly, and you will be able to turn to it automatically when you are feeling stressed," says Marie.

1 Find a safe and comfortable spot to sit. Close your eyes and allow your palms to gently rest on your legs in an upright receiving position.

2 Open your mouth as wide as possible. Slowly take a long inhale, mimicking how the ocean sounds coming into shore. Keep your mouth open wide as you exhale, making the sound of waves going out to sea.

3 Continue for as many repetitions as you need, allowing your belly to rise and fall with the waves of your breathing.

4 As you breathe, gently let any emotions come up. You might cry or laugh. Just continue breathing through it all.

5 When you feel ready, gently open your eyes. Take a moment to tune in to your body. You can ask your body what it might need: a rest, a break, company?

Show Gratitude to Your Emotions

Note a moment when you let your anxiety rule your thoughts and actions. Write a thank-you note to your anxiety, acknowledging it for trying to protect you. It may have come on pretty bossy, sure, but did it have a kernel of good advice for you? What was that advice? After expressing gratitude to your anxiety, explain why you don't need it to be in charge so often anymore.

TRY THIS

Befriend Yourself

When trying to face difficult emotions, give yourself the same support you would offer a dear friend. "Self-compassion is treating yourself with the same care and compassion you would show a loved one," says Silberstein-Tirch. Here are some self-love strategies:

Talk kindly. What would you say to a friend who was experiencing this difficult emotion? Say the same thing to yourself. "Of course this hurts. It's natural you feel this way."

Address yourself by name or use a nickname. "I'm here for you, kiddo!" "It can be comforting to put a hand over your heart or on your own shoulder as you do so," says Silberstein-Tirch.

Create a haven. Find a cozy corner and spruce it up so it evokes feelings of warmth and care. Try to engage all your senses: That might mean painting it a soothing color, keeping fresh flowers, or arranging your softest blanket. "This space can become a retreat, a place of compassion and safety, says Silberstein-Tirch.

What Message Might Your Emotions Be Sending You?

Sometimes a difficult feeling such as anger or sadness is sending you a message about something that's not working in your life. What might your current emotion be telling you? Write a message in a bottle from it here.

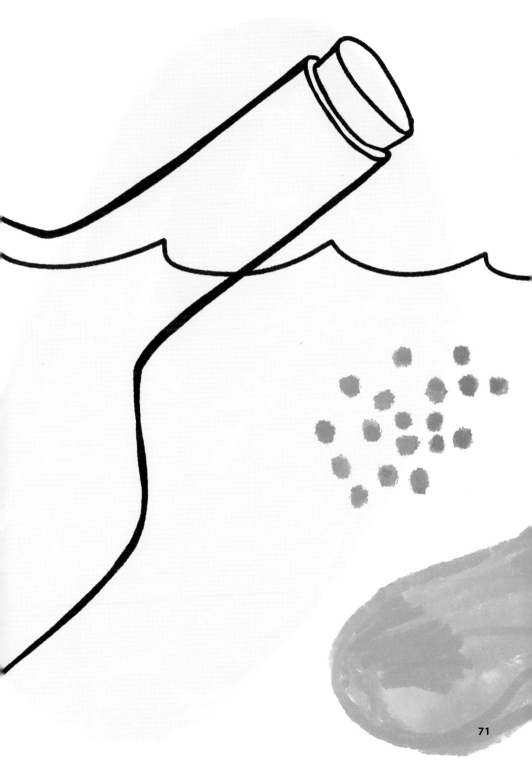

TRY THIS

Next time you are struggling with a challenging emotion such as heartache or loneliness, don't try to slam the door on it. "You might avoid the feeling temporarily, but these emotions will keep getting louder and louder until they get your attention," says Elaine Smookler, a psychotherapist and mindfulness coach. A better idea: Consider welcoming those difficult feelings.

Instead, "invite your demons to tea," suggests Smookler. "Imagine they are guests who are stopping by briefly. All emotions are passing states, after all. You can say, 'Oh look, Anger is here!' Receive them, hear them out, and they will soon be on their way."

This kind of playful approach helps defang the situation, which is why Smookler thinks humor can be so healing. Concludes Smookler: "Humor gives us a lightness that helps us hold all our experiences more easily."

Practice Acceptance

According to psychologists, "meta emotions" are emotions you experience about your emotions. For example, you might feel guilty for feeling angry at your kids or impatient with yourself for feeling anxious rather than brave about a dentist visit. But judging yourself harshly for having an emotion can just compound your suffering, say experts. Practice acceptance instead.

Write about a strong emotion your recently experienced.

....

....

....

....

....

....

....

How did you feel about that emotion? Did you judge yourself for having it?

....

....

....

....

....

....

....

Hint Next time, practice just naming the emotion with acceptance, not judgment.

REJECTION

We have all felt its sting. The pain of rejection is so vivid we feel it physically: We talk about *heartache* or experiencing the chill of a *cold shoulder*. And though romantic jilting might seem the most world-ending (and sell the most ice-cream pints), we find all kinds of brush-offs brutal: the ghosting after the dream-job interview, the social snub, all those left swipes! "Rejections are the most common emotional wound we sustain in daily life," says Guy Winch, Ph.D., author of *Emotional First Aid*.

Rejection straight-up hurts, but it evolved to help us read the room. Being connected to others was once crucial for protection and sharing resources. The pain we feel when we are excluded makes us work hard to prevent being discarded and thus lose those lifesaving bonds.

While there is no instant cure for the pain of rejection, a self-affirmation can help, suggests Winch. "Make a list of your best attributes. I am a good listener. I am loyal. My muffins are unparalleled. Choose one of these attributes and write a one- or two-paragraph reflection on it," says Winch. "Doing so is a powerful reminder to yourself about how much you do have to offer others."

Let's Practice!

List your best attributes below.

....
....
....
....
....
....
....
....
....
....
....
....
....
....
....
....
....
....

Choose an attribute on your list and reflect on this amazing quality of yours below.

TRY THIS

The Gift of Empathy

A longtime meditation teacher and author of *The Wisdom of a Broken Heart*, Susan Piver struggles herself at times. "Once I was wrestling with a painful relationship problem that was really troubling me," Piver recalls. "I went around and around with it. I just couldn't think my way out." Frustrated, Piver sought the counsel of one of her teachers, a Tibetan meditation master.

"I expected this brilliant scholar to give me a doorway to open—advice that would make the problem go away. Instead, he simply told me, 'Think of how much compassion you will have in the future for others who are struggling with this too.'"

"It was an extraordinary moment," says Piver. His remark changed her feelings of isolation into ones of deep connection with others. "I went from thinking, *What's wrong with me? How come I can't fix this?* to realizing everyone suffers. Countless people are struggling in the same way right now. My heart will open to them." Your own difficult times can be a powerful engine of empathy, too.

Let Your Tears Talk to You

Describe the last time you had a really good cry. What caused it? How did you feel before and after?

....

....

....

....

....

....

....

....

....

....

....

....

....

....

....

....

....

Permission to Feel

It is perfectly OK to feel the full range of feelings. There are no wrong answers! Write yourself a permission slip to feel a difficult emotion—perhaps frustration, resentment, or loneliness.

This gives ....

permission to feel ....

....

....

....

without beating myself up.

Refer to your permission slip whenever you feel you "shouldn't" feel that way.

Find the Silver Linings

Recall a time when you experienced a big life upheaval—a loss, a move, a health crisis, or perhaps a divorce.

What negative emotions did you have to live through during that time?

....

....

....

....

....

....

....

Did something positive come out of that difficult time for you?

....

....

....

....

....

....

....

....

....

MANAGE YOUR BIG FEELINGS

practicing emotional regulation

On life's journey, your emotions act as your GPS—they give you valuable information to guide you through challenges. But that doesn't mean you should put them squarely in the driver's seat. You might feel incensed when that jerk with the brimming cart cuts you off in the quick checkout line. But that's not license to hurl your lone gallon of milk, as tempting as that may feel!

Learning to modulate your emotions is a skill that psychologists call emotional regulation. "Emotional regulation does not equal constantly feeling calm, happiness, zen, joy, bliss," explains Britt Frank, L.S.C.S.W., a clinician and author of *The Science of Stuck: Breaking Through Inertia to Find Your Path Forward*. "That's a total misconception. Instead, it is the capacity to maintain choice over your words and actions even in the middle of big feelings. Emotional regulation lets you tolerate and move through difficult emotions without getting stuck in them."

What does emotional regulation look like in practice? The first step can be recognizing and validating the feeling you are having. "Acknowledge you are feeling heartbroken, for example. Don't shame yourself or tell yourself you are wrong for having that feeling," explains Frank. "It can be powerful to simply say to yourself: *This feeling makes sense.* Then, you can move on to consider how to express that emotion productively—writing a letter then burning it or going for a mind-clearing walk or run, for instance."

You can also draw on emotional regulation skills when you are feeling totally overwhelmed and need to soothe yourself, notes Frank. Perhaps you are swamped by a wave of grief but don't want to lose it during a Zoom meeting. Or you are feeling panicky about a work deadline but need to calm down enough to think straight and get the project done.

Developing a roster of go-to strategies, from deep breathing to reaching out to others, can help you better navigate life's inevitable emotional storms.

Let's explore techniques and tips to help you take control.

"The best way out is always through"

—ROBERT FROST

My Self-Soothing Strategies

What comforts you when you need it most? Fill out this list and keep it handy so you can refer to it when you are getting near your red zone.

1. Call a friend
2. Take the dog for a walk
3. Escape into a great book
4.
5.
6.
7.
8.
9.
10.

TRY THIS

If you are overcome with an intense emotion, here's a trick: Simply wait 60 seconds. "Don't instantly follow what the emotion is telling you to do: Don't send that angry text, don't send that flaming email to your boss, don't tell off your mother-inlaw," suggests Amelia Aldao, Ph.D., founder and director of Together CBT. When that minute is up, the emotion and its devilish whispers will likely start to subside, she says. "It might not be gone completely, but it will likely become less compelling. Emotions come on quickly and immediately begin to decay."

Dream Big

Dreams have been called overnight therapy. They can help us process the day's emotions when our stress hormones are lowest.

Write about a vivid dream you had and contemplate its meaning.

....

....

....

....

....

....

....

....

....

....

....

....

....

....

....

....

TRY THIS

Asking for Help Is Essential

"Today, we're trained to be self-sufficient. Work. Parenting. Keeping an Instagram-ready home," says Ashley Womble, M.P.H., a mental health advocate and author of *Everything Is Going to Be OK*. Past generations had extended families and tight-knit communities pitching in. Now, instead of casseroles at the back door, we are more likely to do our own ordering from Grubhub.

But hear this: "You can be blessed and still deserve support. We *all* struggle. Help can come in many forms. It may be seeing a therapist, finding a gym, or delegating some of your tasks," says Womble.

It can be hard to admit you can't juggle everything. So just take that first step. It can be as simple as telling a friend or partner, "I am having a terrible "day," and I just can't do this alone." Start the conversation. "Asking for support is a sign of strength, not weakness. It takes bravery to be vulnerable. In doing so, you show it is OK for others to ask for help too," says Womble.

Move Forward

Ruminating means chewing over a worry endlessly...and fruitlessly. "I think of rumination like a hamster on a wheel, going round and round instead of getting off and moving forward," says Kathy HoganBruen, Ph.D., a clinical psychologist and founder of the District Anxiety Center in Washington, DC. Here's how to get off your own hamster wheel and think more productively.

What am I worried about right now?

....

....

....

....

What is in my control?   **What is not in my control?**

....

....

....

....

....

....

What is a step I can take today to work on the things I can control about my problem?

....

....

....

ENVY

It is arguably the least fun of the seven deadly sins. Envy carries with it a tinge of ill will or resentment toward those we feel closest to. But you are not a bad person to feel it—you are just wired to compare yourself with others, says Sarah Hill, Ph.D., a professor of psychology at Texas Christian University in Fort Worth, Texas. "Our early ancestors kept close tabs on who had the better resources and felt driven to get them for themselves. Those who had that competitive drive survived to reproduce."

The only thing that has changed is what we compete for. Yesterday: the best bison meat. Today: the picture-perfect vacation. Hill's research has found we pay closer attention to those we envy—we gaze at them longer, looking for clues to their success.

Feelings of envy activate regions of the brain associated with physical pain, according to research. Like other forms of pain, envy is a sign that something is wrong and can spur us on to action. It can motivate us to strive for something we think should be ours too.

So take a moment and consider what envy is telling you to work toward. Then swerve back into your own lane and appreciate your own unique goals and gifts.

TRY THIS

Imagine Your Safe Haven

Many survivors of childhood trauma recall coping by building shelters within their own imaginations. They might picture a treehouse where they are safe from the world or conjure up friendly animal guides or imaginary fairies as protectors. Try these exercises to find peace during your own most challenging times.

1. Recruit Helpful Companions

Imagine you're accompanied by a being or beings (they don't need to be human) that make you feel loved and supported. What do they look like? How does it feel to be around them? What are they saying to you?

....

....

....

....

....

....

....

....

....

....

2. Pack a Suitcase

What soothing items have helped you in the past during difficult times? (Think: a photo of a loved one, your softest old sweater, a cup of tea.) Visualize yourself packing those helpful things in a suitcase that's always at your disposal.

....

....

....

....

....

....

....

....

....

3. Design an Inner Refuge

Recall a moment when you felt completely safe. Now imagine a place that makes you feel that same way. What do you see? What relaxing sounds do you hear? What does it smell like? How does it feel? Return to this familiar retreat whenever you're overwhelmed. It is always there for you.

....

....

....

....

....

....

How to Work Through a Difficult Feeling

Reflecting on your feeling in a step-by-step process will help you understand their message.

3

What thoughts are going through my mind right now?

2

What am I feeling in my body right now?

1

Pause and tune in. Record how you feel below.

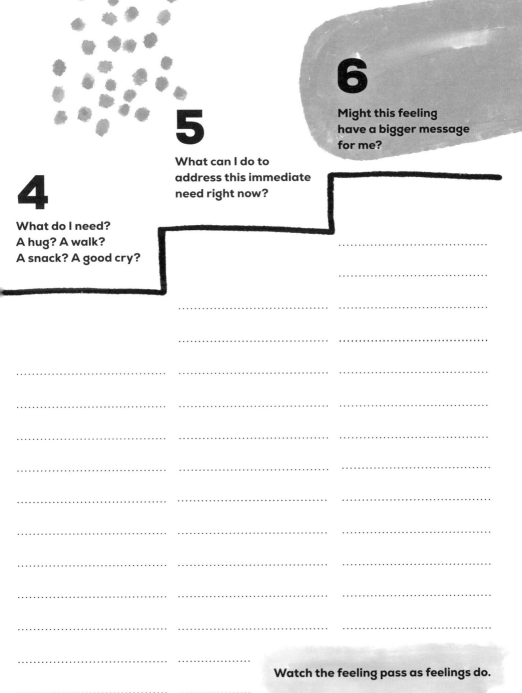

4

What do I need?
A hug? A walk?
A snack? A good cry?

5

What can I do to
address this immediate
need right now?

6

Might this feeling
have a bigger message
for me?

....

....

....

....

....

....

....

....

....

....

....

....

....

Watch the feeling pass as feelings do.

ACCENTUATE THE POSITIVE

CHAPTER
6

cultivating more happiness

Let's face it: Our negative emotions—fury, fear, disdain—tend to suck the oxygen out of the room. We spend much of our time and emotional energy trying to tame them. But as we become more conscious of our emotions, we can actively foster our positive emotions too.

"Happiness is not reserved for those who were blessed with the best genetic code, an easy life, or a supportive upbringing. There's a piece of happiness that is under our own control," says Katherine Nelson-Coffey, Ph.D., associate professor of psychology and director of the Social Connection & Positive Psychology Lab at Arizona State University. "Lots of research in the field of positive psychology shows that when people engage in practices such as expressing gratitude, practicing optimism, and doing acts of kindness for others, it leads to increases in their own happiness."

That doesn't mean you should don rose-colored glasses. "We can savor the good stuff even when life is not perfect," says Harriet Cabelly, L.C.S.W., a therapist and author of *Living Well Despite Adversity*. Cabelly practices what she preaches: When she was undergoing grueling cancer treatments last year, she made a point to tend to her beloved house plants every day. "Intentionally find little bits of joy and hold on to them hard," says Cabelly.

Cultivating positive emotions can help us build more resources to handle challenging times too. When we are happy, we feel more open and freer. "Experiencing positive emotions helps us think more creatively and expansively and makes us more socially inclusive," Nelson-Coffey explains. "When you are feeling buoyant, you might start a new friendship, for instance. That gives you one more person you can call when you are feeling down. These resources mean we can be more resilient in times of stress."

Here is how to tap the power of your positive emotions—even when life is imperfect.

"Happiness is not a state to arrive at, but a manner of traveling"

—MARGARET LEE RUNBECK

Find More Joy

Consider yourself a scientist studying your own positive emotions—
happiness, relief, enthusiasm. Next time you feel delighted, pause
to investigate what situation triggered it and contemplate how you can
coax more of it out of your life.

I felt ....

....

....

....

....

....

My good feelings happened when ....

....

....

....

....

I am going to spend more time ....

....

....

....

....

Good Scentsations

Write about a scent that transports you to a place of joy. That might be cut grass, cinnamon, or dog fur. How would you describe the feelings that smell evokes in you? What happy memories does it conjure up for you?

Follow Your Bliss

Describe a time when you remember feeling utter contentment.

Where were you? ....

....

....

....

....

....

Who were you with? ....

....

....

....

....

What did that feel like in your body? ....

....

....

....

....

....

....

Hint How might you recapture that feeling today?

Go on a Treasure Hunt for Happiness

"We can cultivate our capacity for contentment," says Laura Silberstein-Tirch, director of the Center for Compassion Focused Therapy in New York City, who as a therapist often works with patients on "appreciation training." "We make use of all the senses. One day they make a list of all the things they appreciated through smell. The next day they keep a list of tastes they appreciated." Involving your senses helps you fully savor the experience and wring the most out of the positive feelings they elicit. For the next five days, use one scent each day and go hunting for joy.

Smell ....

....

....

....

....

....

....

Touch ....

....

....

....

....

....

....

Taste ....

....

....

....

....

....

....

Hearing ....

....

....

....

....

....

Sight ....

....

....

....

....

....

....

GET TO KNOW

JOY

Joy is "the good mood of the soul." That's how bestselling author Brené Brown, Ph.D., describes this expansive emotion. Compared to the steadier state of happiness, joy can feel more like a surprise or gift: Colors seem brighter, the world glows afresh. When you experience joy, you may smile spontaneously, even weep giddy tears. "When we find joy inside, we are helped by noticing the sensations in our body like warmth, energy, and peace. With some practice, it feels amazing to stay with this feeling and savor the physical sensations," says Hilary Jacobs Hendel, L.C.S.W., a psychotherapist, emotions educator, and author of *It's Not Always Depression: Working the Change Triangle to Listen to the Body, Discover Core Emotions, and Connect With Your Authentic Self.* Often joy is triggered by a sense of deep connection to something outside ourselves. It is sparked by things we hold most dear. We may feel joy at the arrival of a new baby, the first crocus of spring, a favorite hymn, or a hard-won accomplishment.

Look for little daily moments of joy to build on: watching the sunrise, a heart-to-heart with an old friend, receiving a bolt of good news. "If you look for these micro-moments of joy, you will find them. When you do, acknowledge them as moments of pleasure. Don't put pressure on yourself to hold on to it; don't worry about joy's fleeting nature. Feel it in your body and just let the moment be what it is," says Jacobs Hendel.

⤳ TRY THIS

Make Room for "Microjoys"

In 2020, Cyndie Spiegel lost her mother and her 32-year-old nephew was diagnosed with breast cancer in the same harrowing year. One thing that helped her cope during it all: Making a practice of appreciating the small delights that still surrounded her. A belly laugh with a friend. Making one of her mother's favorite recipes. "Microjoys are easily accessible moments of joy that exist regardless of your current circumstances," says Spiegel, the author of *Microjoys: Finding Hope (Especially) When Life Is Not OK.* "You can hold grief in one hand and joy in the other." Here's her advice for finding your own microjoys.

Stay present. The more you pay attention, the more these joys reveal themselves. "I have a glass prism hung in my window that casts rainbows on the floor. I consciously pause and reflect on this wonder that I otherwise might ignore in my hurrying," says Spiegel.

Take a picture. "I photograph everyday things that make me happy. I have more than 29,000 pictures of mundane delights and extraordinary observations on my phone. When I just need a moment, I scroll through my pictures and find reminders that life is still beautiful despite everything."

Share it. *Freudenfreude* is the term for joy for others' joy. When you find yourself in situations that celebrate others, allow yourself yourself to fully experience that joy for them too.

→TRY THIS

Develop an Appreciative Lens

To get more boosts of good feelings, practice viewing the world through what positive psychology coach Jan Stanley calls "an appreciative lens." Pause and savor what might otherwise be too-fleeting moments of joy, lost in the shuffle of your busyness.

"My living room has large floor-to-ceiling windows facing due east, covered with long, sheer curtains. Each morning, as I walk around the corner from my darkened bedroom, I am welcomed by a warm and beautiful glow coming from the windows, backlit by the sunrise. Some days the glow is white, some days it's yellow, and other days, a pinkish "blush," says Stanley.

"I intentionally make a point to pause and drink in this amazing sight. I say to myself, 'How beautiful. I am so lucky to begin my day in this way.' This sets my appreciative lens in motion for the day, orienting me to be on the lookout for the joyful moments that follow: the aroma of fresh coffee, the laugh of a friend. It is not lost on me that even on cloudy days, the light finds its way through."

Embrace the Bittersweetness

"There's a yin and yang with emotions. You can't have love without risking loss. You can't have gratitude without want," says Silberstein-Tirch.

Write about a time in your life when your negative emotions made your positive ones all the sweeter.

....

....

....

....

....

....

....

....

....

....

....

....

....

....

....

....

"The soul should always stand ajar, ready to welcome the ecstatic experience."

—EMILY DICKINSON

TRY THIS

Play On!

You are never too grown up to play! "I consider play any joyful act in which you forget about time. It has no purpose and no intended result. You're immersed, fully present in the moment," says Jeff Harry, a positive psychology play coach (yes, this is a thing) in Oakland, California. "Play looks very different for everyone."

For adults, taking fun seriously can feel silly, even selfish. We're rusty, self-conscious, afraid we'll look dorky on roller skates—or we're no longer sure how to have fun in the first place. But goofing off is a great way to boost your mood. Here's how to get more playtime in your life.

1 **Think about what you thought was a blast as a kid—**that's probably what you'll most enjoy now. "We all have certain play values. You might have loved creating potions or playing tag," Harry says. Bring the same basic elements into your adult life. Were you an avid tree climber? Give a rock-climbing gym a whirl.

2 **Go out and play.** Spending time outdoors can rev up your spirits and your energy, so let yourself out for recess every day.

3 **Hang out with play experts.** Little kids and pets are Ph.D.s of play. Share in their silliness!

BOOST YOUR BONDS

CHAPTER
7

understanding emotions in close relationships

You spot your BFF's face in a crowded café and feel an instant flush of happiness. You feel green with envy of your sister's success. Your partner leaves dirty pots and pans all over the kitchen (again!), and you pulse with head-to-toe rage. For better or worse, our closest relationships often spark some of the most intense emotions we experience day-to-day. Those feelings can be complicated and confusing to say the least. But being able to better understand your emotions and those of the people around you can pave the way for deeper, more satisfying connections.

Why do our loved one evoke such big feelings? "We are social animals, wired for connection," says Rebecca Williams, L.M.F.T., a marriage and family therapist at Inland Empire Couples Counseling in Southern California. "So we view any perceived rejection or conflict as a threat. It cuts deep." We may also tote emotional baggage from our past into our current relationships, preventing us from seeing or hearing the other person clearly.

"We often bring our unresolved stuff from the families that we grew up in into our current relationship. It's like we are trying to replay the same story to get a different ending," says Williams. "Arguing about who forgot to pick up the dry cleaning might really be about whether we feel overworked, unseen, or unappreciated—and about all the times in our lives we also felt those things."

One way to move away from misunderstanding and toward more satisfying close relationships is to develop greater emotional awareness: *What am I really feeling here and what is really behind that feeling? What might the other person be experiencing underneath their bluster?* That can start by putting aside your old stories and being more present in the here and now with the person right in front of you. According to a 2020 study in the *Journal of Personal Relationships*, subjects who measured higher in the present awareness of mindfulness weathered the day-to-day ups and downs of close relationships with greater satisfaction and calm.

"The strongest relationships are not the ones that have never been tested by conflict or disconnection," says Williams. "The strongest are where you have learned to repair and come back together." The payoff of learning to negotiate emotions in close relationships is enormous. After all, the truest route to joy and happiness can be found in connection with others.

Developing greater emotional awareness lets you show up authentically in the relationships that matter most.

"The capacity to care is what gives life its deepest significance."

—PABLO CASALS

Describe Your Squad

Who are the most significant people in your life? Write their names and your feelings about each in the circles below and on pages 110 and 111.

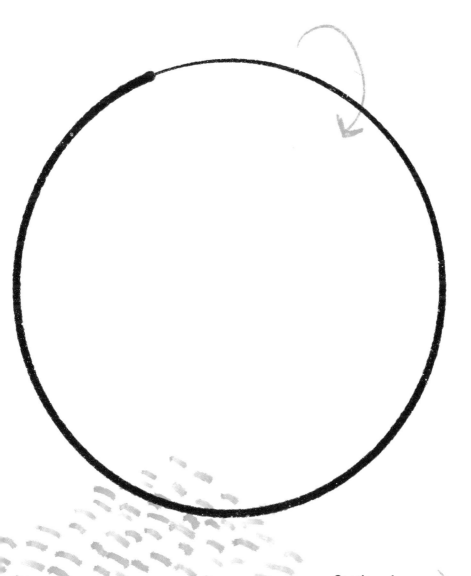

Continued ⟶

Reflect

Who do you feel happiest around?
Is there someone who creates the most
tension in your life? Can you adjust your
time with them accordingly?

Small Acts of Kindness

Helping other people is one of the quickest routes to personal happiness, research has found. Make a point to do a small random act of kindness for someone else once a day this week. You could bring someone a meal, call a friend who is struggling, order pizza for your neighborhood firehouse. Record them here.

SUNDAY

....

....

....

....

....

....

....

MONDAY

....

....

....

....

....

....

....

TUESDAY

....
....
....
....
....
....

WEDNESDAY

....
....
....
....
....
....

THURSDAY

....
....
....
....
....

FRIDAY

....

....

....

....

....

....

....

....

SATURDAY

....

....

....

....

....

....

....

....

Reflect

Reread all the good you did in the world this week! How does this make you feel? How could you make practicing random acts of kindness to others a regular habit?

....

....

....

....

....

....

....

....

....

....

....

....

....

....

....

....

....

Compassionate Conflict

Often arguments are about something much deeper than whose turn it is to take out the trash. Write about a current conflict you are having with someone close to you.

What happened? ....

....

....

....

....

....

....

....

What are your feelings about the situation? Pour them out here. ....

....

....

....

....

....

....

....

....

What does this conflict tell you about what really matters to you?

....

....

....

....

....

....

....

....

TRY THIS

Put On Your Own Oxygen Mask First

Feeling irritated at your relatives? Maybe it's not them. It's you. "If you are hungry, tired, or stressed, research suggests you may be more likely to interpret other people's actions negatively. You are more vigilant for threats," says Amie Gordon, Ph.D., an assistant professor of psychology at the University of Michigan and lab director of the school's Well-Being, Health, and Interpersonal Relationships Lab. This is especially true if you see your loved one mostly at lighting-rod occasions such as wine-soaked holidays. So prepare for that big family gathering by practicing good self-care—and escape for a walk as needed.

TRY THIS

How to Handle Tough Talks When Emotions Are High

While not every discussion has to be a soul-excavation, it's important to be present for "the moments that matter," says Anna Osborn, a marriage and family therapist in Sacramento, California. Here are some expert strategies for handling emotionally charged talks with a partner or loved one.

Reflect on what is really at stake. Your partner won't put down his phone when you are together. Before approaching them, reflect on what bigger issues this behavior may be bringing up for you. Ask yourself, "Why does it really matter to me? What's really at stake?"

Pick a good time. Do not tackle a big talk when you are both tired and cranky. "Sit down over coffee on the weekend or take a walk together to discuss it," suggests Debra Roberts, L.C.S.W., author of *The Relationship Protocol.*

Use "I" statements. Begin by explaining how the situation makes you feel, advises Osborn. "I feel really upset when you put mail all over the kitchen counter because I can't cook. Cooking is how I unwind." Speaking about your emotions in this way encourages empathy and understanding. "A good partner will care about your feelings and want you to feel better," says Roberts.

In contrast, using "you" statements puts the other person on the defensive: "You act like I'm the maid!" "Once the other person gets upset, we have lost them. Nothing is going to get solved," says Roberts.

Silence is golden. Wait for the speaker to take a breath after they stop talking—and don't rush to jump in. That quiet can give them the space to share something big.

Conclude with "we" statements. Suggest possible solutions, but don't dictate them. Using "we" during the problem-solving stage of a conversation reminds the other person you are, after all, a team. "Do you think we should create some new ground rules?"

GRATITUDE

A homemade quiche arrives on your doorstep, and you are overcome with warm feelings. The emotion of gratitude may have evolved as a "powerful social glue," says Gordon. "When we recognize someone else's care and concern for us, we feel grateful. Feeling that emotion then makes us act differently. We value that person more and are motivated to respond in kind."

Making a practice of expressing gratitude can give your romantic partnership a boost. In fact, a study published in the *Journal of Positive Psychology* showed that long-term romantic partners who were assigned to express gratitude to each other regularly over the course of a month reported feeling more positive moods and greater adaptability to their relationship's inevitable ups and downs compared to couples who did not get those instructions.

Why? Feeling appreciated leads to "relationship-building behavior," says Gordon. When your partner acknowledges you, it's validating, and you want to return the favor, she explains; those exchanges tighten your bond.

Who are you thankful for today? Why?

....

....

....

....

....

....

....

Animal Attraction

Our pets can be important sources of love and connection and a proven balm for loneliness. "Pets elicit so much love because we can act like our true selves around them without fear or embarrassment," says Kristyn Vitale, Ph.D., C.A.A.B., an assistant professor of Animal Health and Behavior at Unity Environmental University.

Write about your emotional connection with a beloved animal, past or present.

What emotions did you feel when you were around them?

....

....

....

....

....

....

....

....

....

....

....

....

....

What might that bond have taught you?

....

....

....

....

....

....

....

....

....

....

....

....

....

....

....

....

....

....

....

....

Share Some Love

We often take those we are closest to for granted because we know they are always there for us. Think about a loved one and write about why you feel grateful to have them in your life. What would your life be like without them?

TRY THIS

Empathy is the secret sauce of close relationships. One way to feel more empathy is to practice a form of Buddhist meditation called Loving Kindness, in which you intentionally direct compassionate thoughts to others. Think of someone you love or someone you don't like, or even a stranger on the street. Repeat the following words to yourself as you direct your thoughts to that person. *May you be happy. May you be safe. May you be healthy. May you be at peace.*

AUTHENTIC YOU

CHAPTER
8

fearlessly live your dreams

As you have discovered working through this journal, getting more comfortable with *all* your emotions can be challenging work. But doing so has an enormous payoff: You will live a bigger, more authentic life.

"Emotions are the motivational force that gets us up in the morning, makes us work hard, and makes us care about things," says Jessica Tracy, Ph.D., professor of psychology and director of the Emotions & Self Lab at the University of British Columbia. "The energizing and gratifying feeling of pride when you reach a goal rewards your efforts and perseverance and can push you onward."

Emotions can act as bright flares, illuminating our most cherished values—creativity, community, connection. Next time you have a big emotion, ask yourself, "What is this feeling telling me about what is truly meaningful to me?" Perhaps your boredom is telling you it is finally time to look for a job that uses your untapped creativity. Your sadness is screaming your current relationship is in serious trouble and needs care. Or your deep contentment after getting dirty in your garden all afternoon is telling you to spend more time in nature. Listening to these feelings can help you to build a life that reflects your deepest values.

In turn, having a clear sense of your values acts as a guiding light, steadying you so you can handle emotional bumps along the path. You give the big toast, nerves and all. You risk judgment from others by standing up for a cause you believe in. You follow your heart and leap into a challenging new job.

"The things that are most important to you—starting a family or taking your first dance class—*will* involve uncertainty and discomfort," says Diana Hill, Ph.D., a psychotherapist and host of the *Your Life in Process* podcast. "The ability to be flexible and open and allow for this emotional discomfort to arrive and not run away gives you power and opens possibility."

In the end, true well-being is remaining open and aware and moving toward what is most important to you. "You can become your most authentic self. You don't have to be happy and cheerful and joyful all the time," says Kathy HoganBruen, Ph.D., a clinical psychologist and founder of the District Anxiety Center in Washington, DC. "It's about noticing whatever you're experiencing and being OK with that. That's what leads to real wisdom."

What amazing things will you accomplish if you face all your feelings head on? Take time to reflect on what's most important to you.

"I'm not afraid of storms, for I'm learning how to sail my ship."

–LOUISA MAY ALCOTT

Which of These Values Are Most Important to You? Circle Them.

Adventure	Generosity	Self-Expression
Beauty	Health	Service
Connection	Honesty	Status
Creativity	Justice	Spirituality
Curiosity	Kindness	Tolerance
Fairness	Learning	Wisdom
Family	Nature	

Reflect

Your core values can help guide your daily actions and choices so you can create your most authentic life.

Write about why one of the values you circled on page 127 is meaningful to you.

....

....

....

....

....

....

....

....

....

....

....

....

....

....

What have you done this week that helps you live out this value?

....

....

....

....

....

....

....

....

What can you do next week?

....

....

....

....

....

....

....

....

....

Tattoo You

If you were to get something essential to you tattooed over your heart, what would it be? Draw it here.

What does this tattoo symbolize to you?

....

....

....

....

....

....

....

....

....

....

....

....

....

....

....

....

....

....

....

No Excuses

You don't have to wait until you are perfectly happy and calm to achieve your dreams. (You may be waiting forever!) Replace the word "but" with "and" to prevent negative feelings from standing in the way of what is most important.

Example:

I would love to travel to an exotic destination, ~~but~~ and I am nervous about long flights.

I would love to ....

....

~~but~~ and ....

....

....

....

I would love to ....

....

and ....

....

....

....

TRY THIS

The Beauty of Life Is in the Contrast

Grab your smartphone. Lizzie LaRock, creativity coach and founder of the *Life Feast* podcast, says that taking a "photo walk" can help us appreciate the beautiful complexity of life. "A photo is visually appealing when it has a full range of light, dark, and every shade in between. A photo without much contrast can look and feel flat. The same holds true for life. Our appreciation for the good stuff goes up when contrasted with what might feel more difficult," she says. Her advice for appreciating it all through this lens:

1 **Don't wait for the rainbow!** Take a photo of raindrops through your windshield or reflections in a puddle. You'll be mesmerized by the abstract beauty of the tiny details of an everyday rainstorm.

2 **Be a shadow hunter.** Look for shadows in the morning, late afternoon, or early evening light. Notice how a high contrast between light and dark yields some of the most fascinating photos.

3 **Look for contrasting colors.** Contrast isn't just for black-and-white photos—color opposites can be incredibly vibrant. Victorian houses, neon signs, or even just the bright yellow of a highway line on fresh asphalt can all make interesting contrasting colors to capture.

Capturing these images can give you a fresh perspective on life, she says. "Photographs of storm clouds, raindrops, and lightning are just as awe-inspiring as ones of rainbows and butterflies. Smartphone photography rewards us for rolling with the storms of life and shows us we don't want a life comprised only of sunsets," says LaRock.

Craft a Mantra

Creating a supportive but realistic statement can help you remain undaunted as you move toward your goals. One example: *This is hard but I can do hard things.* Write your mantra here in huge letters.

....

....

....

HOPE

"Hope is the thing with feathers," wrote poet Emily Dickinson: It can keep us aloft even in the most challenging times.

"Hope is an emotion that keeps you going even when things look grim," explains Patricia Bruininks, a professor of psychology at Whitworth University. "Like other emotions, it motivates you toward something. Hope keeps you focused on a potential good outcome."

Hope takes energy to maintain so it is typically focused on something dear to us—a full recovery, a rapprochement, a successful conclusion of a challenging project.

Another reason to hope: It is good for your physical and mental health. A 2020 study in the journal *Global Epidemiology* of some 13,000 people found that a greater sense of hope was associated with better physical health, fewer sleep problems, and a greater sense of purpose.

Many of us may be afraid to hope for something. It comes with the risk of disappointment after all.

One way to kindle more of it in the face of such uncertainty: "When you are faced with an outcome you want to feel hopeful about, it can help to reflect on a past experience when things turned out fine for you, despite the odds," says Bruininks.

Don't Let Fear Hold You Back

Often, achieving something important means doing so despite anxiety or uncertainty. "If you always try to stay within your comfort zone, you may miss the opportunity to engage in what you most value," says Charryse Johnson, Ph.D., founder of Jade Integrative Counseling and Wellness. But if you allow your values not your fears to lead, you expand your comfort zone and become more resilient."

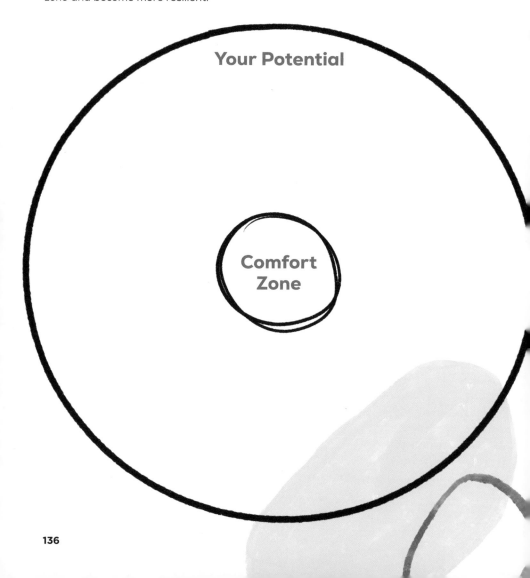

What might you accomplish if fear was not part of the equation?

....
....
....
....
....
....
....
....
....
....
....
....
....
....
....
....
....
....

Be Your Best Self

Write about a time when you felt most alive, most like the true you.
What were you doing? Who were you with?

....

....

....

....

....

....

....

....

....

....

....

....

....

....

....

....

How can you get a little bit of that feeling back in your life today?

....

....

....

....

....

....

....

....

....

....

....

....

....

....

....

....

....

....

....

....

Looking Forward

In working through this journal, you have practiced listening to the wisdom of all your emotions and mining their messages for your life. What big dreams do you have for your future? How might your emotions help guide you there?

....

....

....

....

....

....

....

....

....

....

....

....

....

....

....

....

"Let everything happen to you, beauty and terror. Just keep going. No feeling is final."

—RAINER MARIA RILKE

acknowledgments

Gratitude is a powerful emotion, and I am feeling lots of it right now! Huge thanks to the many experts quoted in these pages. In long phone conversations and thoughtful email exchanges, these therapists, professors, and researchers were amazingly generous with their time and knowledge. Their expertise and patience were crucial in helping me understand and translate the fascinating and ever-changing science of emotions. In many cases, we talked for an hour or more, even if their quoted comments appear here in very abbreviated form.

In addition to the sources cited by name, I would like to thank the other experts I talked to in researching this journal who provided me with valuable insight and greater understanding. Mary Lamia, Ph.D, was particularly generous with her time, expertise, and resources. I am also very grateful for the generosity of Dana Mincer, D.O.; Ann-Marie Kilpatrick, L.C.M.H.C.S.; Emily Urban-Wojcik, Ph.D., Emma McAdam, L.M.F.T.; and Katie Hoemann, Ph.D.

Finally, thanks so much to Elise deSomer for her careful fact-checking and research assistance.

HEARST
HOME

The information in this book is not meant to take the place of the
advice of your doctor or other medical practitioners.

Book design and illustrations by Jessi Blackman

Library of Congress Cataloging-in-Publication Data available on request

10 9 8 7 6 5 4 3 2 1

Published by Hearst Home, an imprint of
Hearst Books/Hearst Communications, Inc.
300 W 57th Street
New York, NY 10019

Hearst Home, the Hearst Home logo, and Hearst Books
are registered trademarks of Hearst Communications, Inc.

For information about custom editions, special sales, premium and
corporate purchases: hearst.com/magazines/hearst-books

Printed in China

978-1-958395-74-5